TRACK AND FIELD

How to Play the All-Star Way

By **Bert Rosenthal**

Introduction by **Mel Rosen**

Illustrated by **Art Seiden**

Photographs by **Jacob Brown**
and **Victah Sailor**

★ An **Arvid Knudsen** book ★

RSVP

RAINTREE
STECK-VAUGHN
P U B L I S H E R S
The Steck-Vaughn Company

Austin, Texas

Acknowledgments

Photographs from the collection of Victah Sailor, pp. 14, 18, 22, 30, and 38. Photograph from the collection of Hershey's National Track & Field Youth Program courtesy of the Lancaster Intelligencer Journal, p. 10, Dan Marsarschka, photographer. Photographs from the collection of Jacob Brown, pp. 4, 13, 21, 25, 26, 29, 34, and 42 Photograph from the collection of Wide World Photos, Inc., p. 6

Published by Raintree Steck-Vaughn Publishers, an imprint of Steck-Vaughn Company

Library of Congress Cataloging-in-Publication Data

Rosenthal, Bert.
Track and field/written by Bert Rosenthal.
p.   cm.—(How to play the all-star way)
"An Arvid Knudsen book."
ISBN 0-8114-5778-8
1. Track-athletics—Juvenile literature. [1. Track and field.]
I. Title. II. Series.
GV1060.5.R64 1994
796.42—dc20   93-23281   CIP AC

Printed and bound in the United States

2 3 4 5 6 7 8 9 0   99 98 97 96 95 94

CONTENTS

Lining up for a practice run

Mel Rosen

INTRODUCTION

Track and field is the greatest sport in the world. In this book, Bert Rosenthal, reporter of track and field for The Associated Press for many years, has written about the history of this sport. He covers the rules governing the sport, its separate events, plus techniques and strategies, and much more. All will help the young reader become a successful athlete.

I feel that athletes, after reading this book, will be able to decide which event or events they may enjoy most. Then, with dedication and practice, they will learn what thousands before them have learned — track and field competition is a wonderful experience.

Young athletes must study each chapter carefully. They must work closely with their coach. They should set goals for the future. Then, maybe someday, they will represent their country in the most important competition in track and field — the Olympic Games.

Good luck to you all!

— *Mel Rosen*
Head Olympic Coach,
USA 1992

Jesse Owens, the greatest track-and-field athlete of his time, served the
United States as its Ambassador of Sports for many years.

A BRIEF HISTORY

Track and field is the most basic of all sports. It includes running, throwing, walking, and jumping. Track and field goes back thousands of years when people lived in caves. Of course, there were no teams or clubs then. There were just men and women, boys and girls, doing what came naturally. Some of these acts involved life or death. People had to run away from stalking animals. Some threw rocks. Others threw sharp pointed sticks to kill charging beasts for food. Fast people escaped their attackers. The slow-footed did not.

In time, throwing for distance became a sport among people. Accuracy was important. One event, spear-tossing, was really the early form of today's javelin competition.

Early humans used to rip branches from trees. They shaped them into poles. With the poles they were able to vault over deep, wide holes in the earth. They could jump over gorges. The poles helped them search for new places to live. They helped them escape enemies. Today, young athletes use fiberglass poles to vault straight upward and over preset heights. The event is called the pole vault.

The city marathon race started way back in 490 B.C. At that time, the Greeks were fighting off the Persian army in the city of Marathon. An unknown soldier was ordered to run to the city of Athens. It was over 26 miles away. His job was to bring the news to the country's leaders. By the time he reached Athens, his feet were cut and bleeding. He was spent. But he had just life enough left to report that the Greeks had won the battle. Then he fell and died. Every marathon run since then is done in his honor.

The Greeks and, later, the Romans met in a series of events they called the Olympic Games. The Olympic Games were named after Olympia, a city in Greece. The games were ended in 394 A.D. after the Romans had beaten Greece in war. The modern Olympic Games started again in 1896.

Over the centuries, the fun and excitement of running, jumping, and throwing was expressed in the play activities of people. It was not until the 19th century that track and field became an organized sport. Various amateur races—sprints, hurdles, and steeplechases— were held at public schools and universities in England.

The first official indoor track meet in the United States took place in New York on November 11, 1868. It was sponsored by the newly formed New York Athletic Club. At about the same time the Intercollegiate Association of Amateur Athletes of America (IC4A) created a meet for colleges and universities.

Interest grew among young men and women to compete in amateur track-and-field events. As a result, the national Amateur Athletic Union, the first ruling body for the sport, was formed. In 1888 the AAU ran the first national championships. These champion- ship events are still held today. The current ruling body is the USA Track & Field.

Another important group for college athletes, the National Collegiate Athletic Association, was formed in 1905. The NCAA held its first track-and-field championships in 1921.

In 1913, track-and-field officials from 16 countries met in Berlin, Germany. They formed the International Amateur Athletic Federation, the governing body of the sport for the world. The IAAF adopts rules for how track-and-field events should be run. It approves world records. It also plans sites and dates for world competitions.

Track and field became a truly worldwide sport with the return of the Olympic Games nearly a hundred years ago. From this new start, the Olympic Games have included almost all the nations of the world. More than 30 different sports competitions are held, including swimming, diving, gymnastics, ice skating, and others. But all sports experts agree that track and field is the most popular.

The Olympic Games are organized by the International Olympic Committee. Competing in the Olympic Games is the dream of young athletes all over the world. Only the best can represent their country at the Olympics. There they go against the best track-and-field athletes of other nations. To win a gold medal is the dream of a lifetime. The honor and glory of being first is earned only by hard work in the cause of a goal. That work starts at a very young age.

Many young athletes run all year round to keep in shape.

QUARTER MILE TRACK

Finish
440 & 880 yd. runs

Start medley

110 yds.

110 yds.
length of arc

Discus

Shot put

Pole vault pit

110 yds.

Start
220, 440,
and 880 yd. runs
200 yd. hurdles

Start
120 yd. hurdle

Start 100 yd. dash

Finish
880 yd. run
100 yd. dash
One mile run
High hurdle

Finish
200 yd.
low hurdle

Finish
220 yd.
medley relay

WHERE TO COMPETE

There is a track-and-field program for boys and girls near you. You can be any shape or size. It does not matter. There is a place for you. You can compete.

There are track-and-field programs all over the nation. Many organizations are devoted to the physical fitness of young people. Many just sponsor track-and-field programs. Many sponsor all sports. Almost all schools, town and city recreation departments, YM-YWCAs, YM-YWHAs, and Police Athletic Leagues, among others, operate sports programs. Get the facts about track-and-field programs near where you live.

Young people with the desire should take part in sports competitions. Sports competitions offer many benefits. Many local stores and businesses support teams and sporting events. Have a relative, teacher, or friend help you sign up.

Among the most important promoters of the sport is USA Track & Field. It is the official governing body of the sport. It is also the operator of the Junior Olympics programs. Boys and girls from 9 through 18 years of age are eligible to enter its youth athletic program. The program is divided into five divisions: Bantam 9-10 years, Midget 11-12 years, Youth 13-14 years, Intermediate 15-16 years, Young Men's/Young Women's 17-18 years.

◄ Rafer Johnson, Olympic gold medalist, teams up for fitness with participants in Hershey's National Track & Field Youth Program.

Girls and boys compete in their own age levels only. More than 1,200,000 young people compete each year in their state regional and national events. Write or call:

USA Track & Field
One Hoosier Dome
Indianapolis, Indiana 46225

(317) 261-0500

Hershey's National Track & Field Youth Program is another important national organization. It holds meets in all 50 states. The organization was founded 16 years ago. It is sponsored by the President's Council on Physical Fitness and Sports. It is open to all young athletes ages 9 to 14. More than a million young people take part each year.

Over the years, many Hershey Youth Program athletes have gone on to set high standards. Mary Lou Retton and Andre Cason are on the alumni list. Mary Lou Retton won the Olympic gold medal in 1984 for gymnastics. In 1979 she took part in the Hershey national final. She placed second in the 50-yard dash.

Andre Cason was the silver medalist in the 100-meter dash and a gold medalist on the 400-meter relay team at the 1993 World Outdoor Championships in Stuttgart, Germany. Cason took part in the 1980, 1981, and 1983 Hershey Youth Program National Finals. Write or call:

Hershey's National Track & Field Youth Program
P.O. Box 810
Hershey, PA 17033

1-800-468-1714

Equipment Needs

You will need an athletic shirt, a pair of running shorts, and rubber-cleated shoes. These make up the basic uniform of a track-and-field athlete. Sweatsuits are used to keep warm before and after meets.

Usually young athletes own two sets of uniforms: one for practice and one for meets.

Your shoes must be kept clean at all times. They should fit snugly.

The javelins, discuses, shots, and hammers are provided by the sponsor organizations at the meets.

The Training Required

Athletes of all ages should keep in shape all year round. In the off-season, swimming, bicycling, and ball playing are good exercises. Many young athletes jog or run all year round. Learn to run on the balls of your feet.

Exercises for strengthening your lungs are important. Your lungs must give your heart a steady supply of air. A simple exercise is to put both arms straight out sideways. Bring the fingertips back to touch your shoulders. Then push them out again in a fist. This will help to train you in deep, steady breathing.

Your coach will advise you on your personal training. Do not use weights without guidance. Each competitor is special. Each person's training is his or her own. But there is more to conditioning than just exercise. Proper diet, rest, and personal hygiene are equally important.

CHAPTER 3

SPRINTING

How often has someone said to you, "Let's race," or "I'll race you?" Once you accept, you are in a sprint race. Sprinting is the purest form of running. It measures your natural speed against the natural speed of your opponent. There is nothing fancy about sprinting. It is done almost all the time in the street or in the playground.

While speed is the most important part in sprinting, strength is also important. Your reactions, your ability to mentally relax and keep a good attitude are also important. Speed is inherited. It cannot be improved by practice. But you can improve your race time by learning how to start properly. You can improve by using proper form throughout your sprint and by finishing your run in the right way. These are the techniques of sprinting.

Size doesn't make a difference in sprinting. There have been champion sprinters under five feet six. Some are as tall as six feet three. The taller sprinters have an advantage because of their longer legs. The shorter sprinters have an advantage, too. They can push harder and quicker out of the starting blocks.

There are three different types of sprints:
1. The short sprint. It is run down a straightaway. The 50-meter, 55-meter, and 60-meter sprints are run on indoor tracks. The 100-meter dash is run outdoors.
2. The 200-meter dash. The runners start just before a curve and have to come around another curve on outdoor tracks.

◀ Evelyn Ashford, former world record holder, was the greatest woman sprinter of all time.

3. The 400-meter dash. The runners circle the track in an outdoor facility. The number of curves or turns will vary in the 200-meter and 400-meter sprints indoors, where the size of the tracks vary.

As a sprinter, you build up strength through lots of workouts and exercises. More muscle strength is needed by a sprinter than for any of the longer races. That strength shows itself at the start of a race when you drive out of the blocks. Your arm and leg movements must be strong. They must give you a powerful start. Since sprint races are so short, a poor start can mean the difference between winning and losing.

Sprinters are like drivers of cars. They take off after waiting for a traffic light. Once drivers have the signal to go, they step on the accelerator. Then they are off and running. When they get moving, they pick up speed. If there is no traffic, they don't slow down until the next traffic light or finish line.

But there are some small differences. As a runner, you often need one stretch during the race where you must let up a little. That could be just before making the final surge to the finish. You must run relaxed. Tense runners never become winning sprinters. It does not matter how much natural speed they have.

Confidence is another important factor. A runner must think he or she will do everything right. By doing so, he or she will win. You cannot go into a race thinking that second or third place will be good enough. You then admit defeat beforehand. No good sprinter can have that attitude.

WORDS FROM A COACH

From the late Bill Lewis, father of Carl Lewis and a former club and high school coach in Willingboro, New Jersey: "Every day we work toward an accomplishment. That is so a kid can go home and say, 'I did something today.' It is important. Teach a kid the mechanics. Teach a kid how to run a race, how to run it right. Then run the race. They'll do it. ... You teach them the best you know how. Then you can only sit back and watch. Be there. That is how we tried to do it with Carl ... and with all the kids."

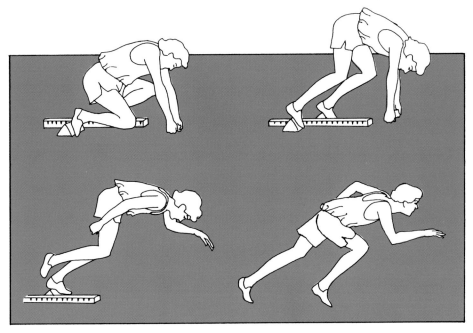

Off and out of the starting block

Your start is important. But there is the point in a race where you have to make a decision. That is when to turn up your speed the most. Then you dash to the finish. The runner who breaks the tape first is the winner. The tape must be broken with some part of the body between the waist and the upper chest.

Sprint races are usually very close. As a sprinter you should learn to lean forward at the finish line. This could give you an edge over your opponents. A runner must run through, not to, the finish line.

Breaking the tape

CHAPTER 4

HURDLING

Hurdling, like sprinting, is something kids do from an early age. When you and your pals jump over bushes or over fences you are hurdling. But these youthful activities are the beginnings of hurdling. Hurdling in track competition is much more scientific.

Like sprinting, hurdling distances vary indoors and outdoors. Indoors, the distances are 50, 55, and 60 meters. Outdoors, where the tracks are larger, the high hurdles distance for women is 100 meters. For men, it is 110 meters. The intermediate distance for both men and women is 400 meters.

In the outdoor races — which are the Olympic distances — hurdlers must clear 10 hurdles. They are set at equal distances apart. The height of the hurdles, however, is different for women than for men. In the 100-meter hurdles, the women must clear 33-inch high hurdles. For men in the 110-meter hurdles, the height of the hurdles is 42 inches. In the 400-meter hurdles, the height for women is 30 inches; for men, it is 36 inches.

As in the sprints, hurdlers must stay in their lanes throughout a race. There is no penalty for knocking over a hurdle. But a runner is disqualified for dragging a foot or a leg alongside any hurdle. The runner must clear it properly. The racer cannot deliberately knock over a hurdle with a hand.

Hurdlers consider themselves hurdlers and sprinters. Hurdling technique and sprinting speed are both important. Unlike sprinters,

◀ Kevin Young is the world record holder of the 400-meter hurdles.

who can be short or tall, hurdlers should be tall. This gives them the advantage of being able to clear a hurdle easier. Size and speed are necessary.

The object of hurdling is to spend the least amount of time in the air. The hurdling action must be smooth. There must be rhythm to it. Forward progress must not be upset. The proper position in clearing

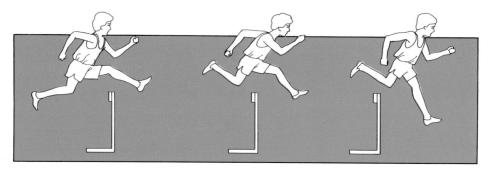

The hurdling action must be smooth.

a hurdle is to extend the front leg forward. The knee must be almost straight. The rear leg should be bent to the outside as it leaves the ground and crosses the hurdle. It must be in a level position parallel with the top of the hurdle.

A forward lean over the hurdles is a must. The trail leg should be "snapped" over the hurdle quickly. This is so the hurdler can get back onto the ground fast and resume running.

Hurdlers must learn to clear the hurdles as closely as possible. There should not be a lot of room to spare. The higher into the air a hurdler goes, the longer it takes to get back onto the track. This costs valuable time. A backward lean over the hurdles will slow a hurdler down. The more forward the hurdler's lean, the better. He or she must have good balance. All this enables a hurdler to begin the drive toward the next hurdle.

Arm action also is important in hurdling. Most hurdlers tend to form their own style of carrying their arms. The most common form is one arm forward and the other arm back. Others swing one arm out to the side. Still others have both arms forward. Whichever style

Hurdlers have speed and quick, easy movement. ▶

gives a hurdler the best balance should be used. But not if it gets in the way of speed.

With practice, a hurdler will know how many steps are needed between hurdles. In the 400-meter hurdles races the distance between hurdles is longer. Hurdlers can go offstride. They must learn to make up for a mistake. They must be prepared to clear with either leg. A 400-meter hurdler, like a long sprinter, must pace him or herself well.

Because hurdlers have both speed and quick, easy movements, they also can be good jumpers. They are usually good long jumpers, triple jumpers, or high jumpers.

CHAPTER 5

RELAY RACING — TEAMWORK RUNNING

Relays are among the most popular track-and-field team events. They allow more athletes to take part in each race. Relays use four runners on each team each usually running an equal distance.

Relays are run at various distances. The most popular relay distances are 400 meters and 1,600 meters. These are the two distances that both men and women run in the Olympics.

While speed is important in relay racing so is baton passing. Three good baton handoffs can greatly increase a team's chance of winning a race. Poor handoffs can cost the team the race.

Baton passing is a skillful act. It requires lots of practice and exact timing. Movement must be constant. Dropping the baton must be avoided. Running out of the 20-meter passing zone will cause loss of the race.

If the baton is dropped in the passing zone, either runner may pick it up. If it is dropped outside the zone, the runner who dropped it must pick it up. A runner must finish a race with a baton. Without a baton, the team loses.

There are two basic ways of passing a baton. One is the blind pass. The other is the visual pass.

The blind pass is used in shorter races. The runners receiving the baton do not look back when the baton is placed in their hands. The

◄ Carl Lewis is the greatest sprinter and long jumper of all time. Here he is competing in a relay event.

timing of this pass must be perfect. It requires many hours of practice.

The two runners taking part in the pass must work out the spot they will be in at the handoff. The spot depends mainly upon the speed of the runner receiving the baton. The burden of the handoff lies with the receiver. The receiver knows that the runner handing off the baton has just run hard and is tired. So the receiver must not make the previous runner run farther than necessary.

The best position for a blind handoff is with both runners running at top speed. The pass of the baton should be made with the runners as far apart as possible. Each runner fully extends the arm — one forward, the other back. The pass generally is made from the runner's right hand to the receiver's left. It can be made the opposite

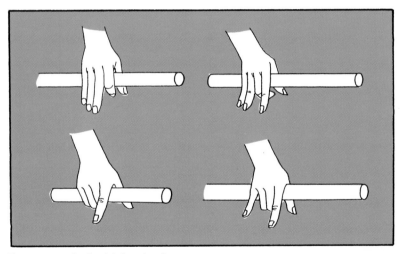

Four ways to hold the baton

way, but it must be practiced. When the receiver gets the baton, it is quickly switched to the other hand. Then it will be ready for the next pass.

The receiver's hand should be extended with the palm up. This is so that the baton will have less chance of falling to the ground. The

Baton passing is a skillful act.

baton should then be gripped tightly. This will prevent the runner from dropping it.

Baton passing is not as important in longer races. But it must be done properly. In the longer races, the visual pass is used.

In this case, the receiver watches the runner coming in. The receiver tries to know the speed of the incoming runner. He or she must pace him or herself correctly. The idea is for the fresh runner to get the baton. Then the fresh runner begins running as soon as possible.

In longer relay races a team can fall far behind. But one runner should not try to make up the distance too quickly. This can result in a runner going all out in the first part of the relay leg with nothing left for the second half. That's why runners should learn to pace themselves. It is the same as in an individual race.

Relays are a very important part of a team's season. One of the most popular relay carnivals in the country is the Penn Relays. Others are the Drake Relays, the Texas Relays, and the Kansas Relays. They attract thousands of runners each year. The runners range from grade school athletes to masters and handicapped runners.

Distance running involves a wide range of distances and events.

DISTANCE RUNNING AND ENDURANCE EVENTS

Distance running and endurance events are not part of any youth program's meets. Young boys and girls are not strong enough for them. They should not try to race in them. But these races are important track-and-field events. They are popular worldwide. One day you may take part.

Distance running involves a wide range of distances and events. Any race longer than 2,000 meters is considered a long-distance event. This includes the 26-mile, 385-yard marathon. There is even an ultra-distance race of 100 miles. But the most celebrated is the marathon race. The men's marathon, by tradition, is the final event on the Olympic program.

Middle-distance races range from 800 meters to 2,000 meters. The most important middle-distance race is the mile.

Frank Shorter of the United States won the 1972 Olympic marathon. Ever since then, marathon running has been very popular. Shorter's win was the first by an American marathoner in the Olympics since 1908. It renewed interest in running all over the nation.

Before 1972, there were very few marathons held in the United States. Now there is a marathon held almost every weekend. The famous Boston Marathon and the New York City Marathon are among the two most popular marathons in the world.

Most marathoners want to run the Boston Marathon. It has a rich history. To enter, runners must meet an entry standard set by the organizers. The New York City Marathon has no entry standards. It gets more marathoners than any marathon in the world. The main reasons are its location and television.

Getting ready for a marathon or a long-distance race is much different than for a middle-distance race. Marathoners, for example, generally run at least 100 miles a week. Some run close to 200. Middle-distance runners do not have to run that many miles. They train for speed more than strength and endurance.

Both middle-distance and long-distance runners must learn pacing. It is important for them to know whether they have a strong finishing kick. Can they wait until late in a race before making their big move? Must they run hard early? Must they establish a big lead to fend off the late kickers? These are the qualities needed for proper pacing.

The distance race of most interest is the mile. For years, there was a great mental block in track. No one could believe running the mile in less than four minutes was possible. Finally, on May 6, 1954, in Oxford, England, a lanky British medical student, Roger Bannister, cracked the four-minute mark for the first time. He clocked 3:59.4. Since then, the record has been lowered to under 3:50. New Zealander John Walker, the 1976 Olympic gold medalist in the 1,500-meter race, did it first.

The marathon and the mile are the most famous of the distance races. But the most unique is the 3,000-meter steeplechase. In this race, runners must go over 28 dry hurdles (four per lap) and seven

Cross-country racing requires strength and endurance.

water jumps (one per lap). Dealing with the water jump takes a special technique.

At the water obstacle, the hurdle is in front of a 12-foot-long pool. The pool is 2 1/2 feet deep. It is just in front of the barrier and slopes up to ground level. A runner can place one foot on top of the hurdle. He or she can push off and land beyond the pit. But the runner usually lands with one foot in the pit. Some runners prefer to clear the barrier in regular hurdles fashion. Then they land in the pool of water.

Steeplechasers can be disqualified for going around a water jump. They also can be disqualified for failing to go through or over the water, or for trailing a foot or a leg alongside any hurdle.

Long-distance running is fun to watch. Watchers get the chance to study all the strategies used by the runners. The longer the race, the more chances for a runner to put on surges. The runner will try to upset his or her opponents. This provides the fans with different stages of excitement and interest.

LONG JUMPING

A great long jumper needs speed, jumping ability, and technique. Speed is most important when coming down the runway. It enables the jumper to achieve top momentum when taking off. But speed must be used properly. While racing toward the takeoff board, the jumper must not break stride. He or she must take off on the proper foot. On the approach, the jumper also must hit the takeoff board at the front. He or she must not pass the plane. A jumper going beyond the plane is called for a foul. On the other hand, jumpers taking off too far back lose valuable distance on their jump.

Once in the air, a jumper must have good body control. The body must be pushed forward for the best possible distance. In the air, jumpers use different styles. One popular style is the "hitchkick." Another style is the "hang" or "tuck" technique.

In the hitchkick, jumpers seem to be running in air by alternating their leg action. The lead leg is extended forward. Then it is swung backward. Again, the takeoff leg comes forward. The lead leg then rejoins the takeoff leg in front of the body for the landing.

In the hang position the knees are tucked under the body in mid-flight. The hang position is the easiest to learn because it is the simplest to do. The jumper's legs are not fully extended during the jump. It is harder to get great distance with this kind of style. But it is used by many jumpers who cannot master the hitchkick.

Another common style is a technique between the hitchkick and hang position. In this technique the body is nearly erect, and the arms are flung overhead.

◄ Jackie Joyner-Kersee is the greatest woman athlete of all time in track and field.

The final phase of the jump is the landing. Jumps are measured from the nearest mark in the sand-filled landing pit. It is important for the jumper not to fall back or sit down in the pit upon landing. The jumper must reach with the legs for every possible quarter inch. A jumper should try and make sure the knees and hips fold forward.

Any loss of distance because of a faulty landing can make the difference between winning or losing. It can be the difference between breaking or just missing a record.

GETTING BETTER

At 9 years old, Jackie Joyner-Kersee signed up for a dance program at a local community center. It was in her home town of East St. Louis, Illinois.

"The instructor cared for me a lot. He felt that one day I would be on Broadway," she said. "Unfortunately, the person died. That is when I turned my attention to track and field."

Remembering when she began she said, "I thought I could make the Olympic team but not win gold medals. I wanted to do it all. I wasn't the best. There were a lot of girls better than me. But I could see that each day I was getting better." Today she is the best. She won Olympic gold medals in 1988 and 1992 in the heptathlon events. In 1988 she was also an Olympic gold medalist in the long jump.

Long jumping has produced some of the most memorable names in track-and-field history: Jesse Owens, Ralph Boston, Bob Beamon, Carl Lewis, Mike Powell, and Jackie Joyner-Kersee. The legendary Owens improved the world long jump record to 26 feet 8 1/4 inches on May 25, 1935. On that day he also tied the world record for the 100-yard dash. He set world records for the 200-meter dash and 220-yard low hurdles.

Owens' long jump record lasted more than 25 years — until August 1960. That was when Ralph Boston raised it to 26 feet 11 1/4 inches. In 1961, Boston twice improved the record. He became the first man to jump 27 feet. He broke his own record two more times. Then he matched it once more before he retired.

The world record stood at 27 feet 5 inches until October 18, 1968. Bob Beamon broke this record by nearly two feet. He made this unbelievable jump at the Olympic Games in Mexico

City. Beamon sailed through the air and won the Olympic gold medal. He leaped 29 feet and 2 1/2 inches.

Carl Lewis came along in the early 1980s. He became the most consistent jumper in the world. He has recorded more 28-foot jumps than anyone in history. He had a 65-meet, 10-year winning streak that was not broken until 1991. At the World Outdoor

Once in the air, the long jumper must have good body control.

Championships in Tokyo, Japan, Mike Powell broke Bob Beamon's 23-year-old record. Powell made a leap of 29 feet 4 1/2 inches. In that same meet, Carl Lewis had three jumps of 29 feet or better. That was the first time anyone had jumped beyond 29 feet more than once in a meet. Lewis also made another jump that was one-quarter inch short of 29 feet.

The Fosbury flop is the dominant style in high jumping.

CHAPTER

8

JUMPING FOR HEIGHT

High jumping and pole vaulting are events in which competitors jump for height. They are two of the most exciting events in track and field. Both require great speed. They also require jumping ability and strength. High jumping and pole vaulting require the ability to bring all bodily skills into action at the same time. Both are associated with daring and high barriers.

Most youth programs do not offer these events in their competitions. These harder events are entered at the high school level. But they are important to know about.

The High Jump

Charles Dumas of the United States cleared 7 feet in the high jump in 1956. He became the first athlete to jump beyond that special height. It was a major accomplishment.

Other jumpers improved on Dumas' world record over the next thirty years. But no one was able to overcome the next barrier — 8 feet — until 1989. Then Javier Sotomayor of Cuba set the world record.

The biggest change in high jumping was a new style of jumping, the Fosbury flop. It got its name from Dick Fosbury, the United States jumper who won the 1968 Olympic gold medal. Fosbury's win made the "flop" famous. It was widely accepted. There are very few jumpers who use any other technique now.

In the "flop," the jumper goes over the barrier head first. With the back to the bar, he or she lands on the shoulders.

The straddle is the old style of high jump. It is still used by a small number of jumpers. In this style the athlete extends the lead leg upward toward the crossbar. The athlete then drapes him or herself face downward and parallel to the bar at the height of the jump. He or she lands on a side or back onto the foam rubber mat.

Knocking the bar off means a miss in high jumping and the pole vault. Three straight misses at any height means a high jumper or a pole vaulter is out of the competition. The heights at which to jump are chosen by the competitor above the minimum set by the meet officials. Jumpers and vaulters also have the choice of passing at certain heights. They can choose to compete at higher heights. If jumpers or vaulters tie, the competitor with the fewest misses wins.

The Pole Vault

More progress has been seen in the pole vault than in the high jump. The new springy fiberglass pole during the 1960s has allowed vaulters to reach greater heights.

Cornelius Warmerdam of the United States achieved the first 15-foot vault in 1940. It was a record hard to believe at the time. He used an old bamboo pole. This primitive piece of equipment seems odd today. Warmerdam's record stood until 1962. Then, another American, John Uelses, made the first 16-foot vault outdoors. He used the new fiberglass pole.

Only 18 months later the record was broken again. John Pennel, also of the United States, cleared 17 feet. Then, in 1978, Christos Papanicolaou of Greece pole-vaulted 18 feet. The 19-foot barrier was scaled for the first time in 1981 by Thierry Vigneron of France.

Finally in 1991, Sergei Bubka of Ukraine broke the 20-foot barrier both indoors and outdoors. Bubka is considered the greatest vaulter of all time. He is a master at breaking the record in small bits. He

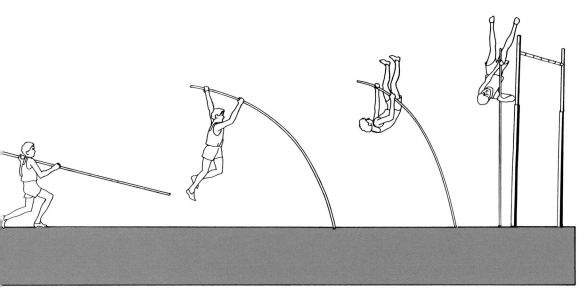

Pole vaulters develop their own styles for reaching their goals.

does it a quarter-inch or a half-inch at a time. Each time he broke the record, he received bonus money from his sponsor, a shoe company.

Style

It is important for high jumpers and vaulters to develop their own styles. The styles have to be ones that feel most comfortable. Trying to copy someone else's method can result in injury. Some jumpers prefer to start their run-ups from the left side. Others prefer the right side. Still others approach the bar almost straight on. The distance of the run-up also varies.

Pole vaulters also have different length run-ups. Some use light poles; others use heavier ones. And some have higher grips on their poles than others. It's all a matter of comfort. Everything has to go together at the same time to get the best effort. Reaching the next height has to be the vaulter's personal goal. It is not always important to go after a record.

Pole vaulters are much like gymnasts. Upper body strength, balance, and courage are important.

THE GREAT THROWING EVENTS

Track and field has four throwing events. They are the shot put, discus, hammer, and javelin. All of them require strength, speed, mind and body working together, and balance. Each event uses special equipment of different sizes and shapes.

The Shot Put

The shot is a solid ball of iron, brass, or any metal not softer than brass. A man's shot weighs 16 pounds. A women's shot weighs 8 pounds 13 ounces.

A shot-putter must use any body motion to put, or push, rather than throw, the shot. He or she starts from a stationary position. The one hand used for putting must not drop below its position at the start of the motion.

Shot-putters launch the ball from a 7-foot wide ring. They may touch the inside of the raised toeboard at the front of the shot-put circle. But if they touch the top of it or the area beyond the ring, it is a foul.

Putting is really pushing the shot. It may look easy, but it is not. In addition to strength, the shot-putter must use speed and muscles that work together. He or she must be able to release the shot in one hard, fast motion across the circle.

◄ Dan O'Brien is holder of the world record in the decathlon.

Because of the weight of the ball and the difficulty in putting it far, shot-putters are among the sport's biggest athletes. Many of them are football players.

Shot-putters often work with weights, trying to build their strength. The extra bulk helps add to the distance of a throw, provided the form is correct.

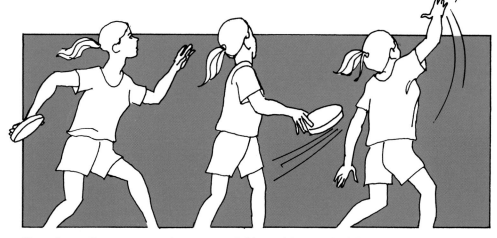

The discus thrower needs a powerful hand to control the platter.

The Discus

The discus is much lighter than the shot. It is shaped like a plate and is 8 1/2 inches in diameter. For college men, the weight of the discus is 4 pounds 6.5 ounces. For high school boys, the weight is 3 pounds 9 ounces. For college women, the weight is 2 pounds 3.2 ounces. The discus is made of wood or other suitable material, with a metal rim.

Many shot-putters also throw the discus. But the physical strength for the two events are different. The discus thrower needs a strong set of shoulders and legs. He or she also needs a powerful hand to control the platter. And, he or she needs a long, sturdy arm with which to sling it.

The discus circle is 8 feet 2.5 inches in diameter. Discus throwers begin by facing the back of the throwing circle. They then take 1 1/2 quick turns before releasing the platter. If the thrower steps on or beyond the circle before the discus lands, the throw is a foul.

The discus event has produced one of the greatest athletes of all time, Al Oerter of the United States. He is the only athlete to have won four gold medals in a single track-and-field event at the Olympics. Oerter won his first Olympic title in 1956. He then followed with victories in 1960, 1964, and 1968.

The Hammer

Only a few high schools, notably in the New England states, include the hammer throw in their field event programs. But it is an important event. It is included in most college programs and the Olympics. Like discus throwers, hammer throwers compete from inside a steel wire or fiber netting cage. Like the shot put, the hammer, for men, weighs 16 pounds. But, unlike the discus and the shot, the hammer is attached to a length of wire four feet in length. It is gripped with both hands.

Hammer throwers spin around 3 or 4 times before releasing the hammer. Spinning with great speed results in greater distance for the throw. Centrifugal force drives the hammer outward from the center of the spin.

Hammer throwing is very difficult. The thrower must spin with great force and keep control of the hammer. The athlete must keep the hammer as far away from the body as possible. All of these techniques help increase the distance.

The Javelin

The shot, discus, and hammer have changed very little over the years. But the javelin has changed many times. Some javelin throwers throw far longer than a football field, more than 300 feet or 100 yards. Some track stadiums are not equipped to handle throws of such distance. At those distances, javelins land on the track.

The surface of the shaft of the javelin must be without grooves or ridges. It must not have holes or roughness. The finish must be uniform and smooth throughout.

Speed and quickness are important to the javelin thrower.

Javelins are the lightest of the four throwing implements. Men's javelins weigh about 1 pound 12 ounces. They are about 8 1/2 feet long. Women's or girl's javelins weigh 1 pound 5 ounces. They are 7 1/2 feet long. Because the javelin is lighter, javelin throwers do not have to be as bulky as the other throwers. Speed and quickness are more important.

The javelin is also the only one of the four throwing events to use a runway. The runway is about 100 feet long. Javelin throwers come down the runway carrying the javelin about shoulder length. The javelin must be released overhand. It cannot be hurled or slung.

The javelin does not have to stick in the ground when it lands. But the javelin's point must come down first. Throws are measured from the mark made by the point to the intersection of the sector lines on the foul line.

GETTING READY FOR THE BIG EVENT

You must have your mind and body ready for the big event. A poorly prepared athlete will not perform well. A well-prepared athlete will perform up to or above what is expected.

Every athlete has his or her own routine before competition. But it should meet the coach's guidelines. Your routine should work. The main concern for an athlete before a meet is to be relaxed. You should be under control. You should be confident. You should be physically ready to perform. Without this mix, you will not perform at your best.

Getting ready for a meet begins the night before. As an athlete, you must get the proper amount of sleep. If you need only 6 hours of sleep, that's fine. If you need 8 or 10 hours, you should get that.

On the day of a meet, eat a good meal a few hours before your competition. Meat and nuts are good for protein. Eat early enough to allow for proper digestion. Never compete on a full stomach. For carbohydrates, eating pasta the day before the competition is fine.

Before a competition, it is important to discuss your opponents' strengths. You also need to talk about his or her weaknesses. What do you think your opponents are likely to do? In running events, for example, does your opponent like to run the race hard early? Does he or she coast in the middle? Does he or she have a big finishing

SCORING

Track and field is basically an individual sport. But team scoring is sometimes called into play. For example, in the Olympic Games, the best nation in track and field is determined by the highest total of gold, silver, and bronze medals.

In the United States, scoring is done at high school, college, and national championship meets. Points are assigned to a certain finishing position. The points given are 10, 8, 6, 4, 2, or 1 for the first six places. Again, the team with the most points wins.

There are exceptions, however. In cross-country, road running, and race walking, the first-place finisher receives one point. The second-place finisher gets two, and so on. In this case, usually only the scores of the first five finishers for each team are totaled. The team with the fewest points wins. Teams with fewer than five competitors do not score as a team. If two athletes finish in a tie for a position, the points are divided.

Teams with more than five competitors can use their extra competitors as "pushers." For instance, in a team meet, team A has places 1, 3, 5, 10, 11, 14, and 15; team B has 2, 4, 12, 13, and 17; and team C has 6, 7, 8, 9, and 16. Team A would be the winner with its first five finishers totaling 30 points. Team C would be second with 46 points. Team B would be third with 48 points. In this case, team A's sixth-place and seventh-place finishers forced C's fifth man to be 16th and B's fifth man to be 17th.

kick? Does your opponent run hard from the start and try to hold on all the way? Does your opponent like to sit behind the pacesetters early? Will he or she then come on with a rush at the end?

Knowing how to pace yourself against your competitors is important. Knowing your own ability is of equal importance. It can help you figure out a strategy for the race. You then can apply your best strategy to win.

In long-distance road races the courses are all different. It is important to see the layout. Look at the course a day or two before the race. Get to know all the turns, curves, uphills, and downhills. Know all other special parts of the area.

On competition day, athletes should begin warming up about 45 minutes before their event. The routines should be mainly stretching and jogging. Hard resistance exercises, such as push-ups, should be avoided. On a cold day, more warm-ups are needed than on a hot day. This is necessary in order to loosen up the muscles.

Field event athletes are given time to warm up with their special equipment. For example, they take practice throws in the shot-put ring. Jumpers make run-throughs in the long jump and triple jump pits. Throwers hurl the discus, javelin, or hammer. Pole vaulters practice takeoffs down the pole vault runway.

Some athletes try to scare their opponents. Some do it by getting off long practice throws in the shot put. Some do it by jumping far in the pits. Once in a while, these tricks work. But they must be used sparingly. Too much use could work against the athlete using the scare trick. It could drain him or her of too much energy.

Field event athletes warm up before meets with their special equipment.

The Coach

Some athletes benefit from a coach's pep talk just before competition. Good coaches talk in an easy manner. Too much excitement or eagerness causes athletes unneeded pressure.

Some athletes just need a simple pat on the back. Some need words of encouragement. Others might just need some simple reminders about strategy or technique. Coaches try to develop the type of mental attitude that helps athletes perform at their best. Before the big event, last-minute instructions are usually comforting.

Final Word

Athletes competing in track-and-field events find many benefits. There is a sense of personal accomplishment. You do not always win. But you do steadily improve on your best efforts. There is the sense of being part of a team. Perhaps you will help your team win a prize. Being part of a team sport generally leads to friendships. Many friendships will last a long time. Being a talented athlete can win you many awards. It can possibly even lead to making an Olympic team someday. Who knows? A gold medal could be in your future.

GLOSSARY

Anchor: The fourth and final runner on a relay team

Baton: The hollow cylinder passed from one runner to the next runner in a relay race

Blind pass: The act of passing the baton from one runner to another without the receiver looking back for the baton.

Fosbury flop: A high jump style developed by Dick Fosbury of the United States,

the 1968 Olympic champion. Jumpers using this method go over the bar head first with their backs to the bar. They land on their shoulders.

Hang technique: A style used by long jumpers. It is done with the knees tucked under the body in mid-flight.

Hitchkick: The long jumpers' art of "running in air" by alternating leg action

Hurdle: The barrier a runner

must clear during a hurdles race

Leadoff Runner: The first runner on a relay team

Long-distance races: Races of more than 2,000 meters

Marathon: The longest track-and-field event in the Olympic Games—26 miles, 385 yards

Middle-distance races: Races ranging from 800 meters to 2,000 meters

Olympic Games: A competition among nations in several sports held every four years. Track and field is the most popular Olympic sport.

Pace: The ability to regulate one's rate of speed

Passing zone: The 20-meter distance in which the baton must be exchanged during relay races

Pusher: Used in cross-country, road racing, or race walking team competition. The pusher is an athlete who does not finish among his team's top five. The pusher does not count in the scoring. But the pusher could prevent an opposing team member from getting that point for a position. For example, if team A's first five finishers are one through five and its sixth runner finishes sixth, the pusher prevents team B from getting sixth place, pushing its first finisher to seventh.

Relay racing: An event in which four athletes from the same team most often take turns running equal distances around the track exchanging a baton

Sprints: The shortest races in a track meet ranging from 50 meters to 400 meters

Steeplechase: A race in which a runner must clear hurdles and water jumps placed along the course

Straddle: A style of high jumping. The athlete extends the lead leg upward toward the crossbar. He or she then drapes himself face downward and lands on a side or back.

Takeoff board: The area at the end of a long jump or triple jump runway at which point the competitor cannot cross before beginning his or her attempt. Crossing the line results in a foul.

Toeboard: The raised area at the front of the shot put ring. A thrower may touch the inside of the toeboard. But if the thrower touches the top of the toeboard or the area beyond the ring, it is a foul.

Triple jump: A jump for distance consisting of a hop, a stride, and a jump

Visual pass: The act of passing the baton from one runner to another during a relay race. The receiver looks at the incoming runner and sees the baton. This method is generally used in longer relay races.

FURTHER READING

Gutman, Bill. *Track & Field*. Marshall Cavendish, 1990

Merrison, Tim. *Field Athletics*. MacMillan, 1991

Sandelson, Robert. *Track Athletes*. MacMillan, 1991

Stanley, Jerry W. *The Track & Field Training Diary: Your Personal Workout Record*. Sports Diary Publications, 1993

Wright, Gary. *Track & Field: A Step-By-Step Guide*. Troll Associates, 1990

INDEX